James Dean

SUTTON POCKET BIOGRAPHIES

Series Editor C.S. Nicholls

Highly readable brief lives of those who have played a significant part in history, and whose contributions still influence contemporary culture.

SUTTON POCKET BIOGRAPHIES

James Dean

WILLIAM HALL

SUTTON PUBLISHING

First published in the United Kingdom in 1999 by
Sutton Publishing Limited · Phoenix Mill
Thrupp · Stroud · Gloucestershire · GL5 2BU

British Library Cataloguing in Publication Data

A catalogue record for this book is available from the British Library

ISBN 0-7509-2123-4

 ALAN SUTTON™ and SUTTON™ are the
trade marks of Sutton Publishing Limited

Typeset in 13/18 pt Perpetua
Typesetting and origination by
Sutton Publishing Limited.
Printed in Great Britain by
The Guernsey Press Company Limited,
Guernsey, Channel Islands.

*For my old friend Mike Maloney,
who made the memorable
pilgrimage with me to Fairmount,
Indiana, where the story of
James Dean begins and ends.*

C O N T E N T S

ACKNOWLEDGEMENTS

The author would like to express his gratitude to the editors, proprietors and columnists of numerous newspapers and magazines consulted, as well as to the authors of the biographies and other books of reference cited in the bibliography.

If the publisher and the author have unwittingly infringed copyright in any picture or photograph reproduced in this publication, we tender our sincere apologies and will be glad of the opportunity upon being satisfied as to the owner's title, to pay an appropriate fee as if we had been able to obtain prior permission.

CHRONOLOGY

1931	**8 February**. James Byron Dean born in Marion, Indiana
1936	Moves with his parents to Los Angeles
1940	**14 July**. His mother (Mildred) dies. 'Jimmy' returns to Mid-West to be raised by his uncle Marcus and aunt Ortense Winslow in Fairmount, Indiana
1941	Gives a moving performance in local church play *To Them that Sleep in Darkness*
1943	Enters Fairmount High School, Indiana
1945	Dean's father remarries, causing him fresh isolation
1949	**16 May**. Graduates from High School, then moves to California to enrol at UCLA
1950	Begins acting with James Whitmore's Little Theatre Group, and picks up small parts in TV and commercials
1950–5	Appears in thirty-four TV productions, including *The Dark, Dark Hour* with Ronald Reagan
1951	Small parts in comedy films *Sailor Beware*, starring Dean Martin and Jerry Lewis, and

Samuel Fuller's Korean war drama *Fixed Bayonets*. Heads for New York and wins minor role on Broadway in *See the Jaguar*

1952 Bit part in *Has Anybody Seen My Gal?* in Hollywood. Joins the Actors Studio in New York

1952–4 Appears in productions and staged readings on Broadway, off-Broadway and in-house performances at the Studio

1954 Wins Daniel Blum Theatre World Award for Promising Personality of 1953/4. Stars in *Women of Trachis* at the Cherry Lane Theatre, New York, opposite Eli Wallach. Acclaimed role in Broadway play *The Immoralist* leads to screen test for Warner Bros. Major screen debut in *East of Eden*, resulting in critical and public acclaim, and an Academy Award nomination

1955 The definitive role that personified restless American youth in *Rebel Without a Cause*. Sprawling Western saga *Giant* that won him a second Oscar nomination. Friendship with Elizabeth Taylor, and romance with Ursula Andress

1955 **17 September**. Films a 30-second safe-driving commercial for the National Safety Council, with actor Gig Young

1955   **30 September**. 5.45p.m.: James Dean dies at the wheel of his Porsche Spyder, at more than 100 mph, in a head-on collision on Highway 466 near Bakersfield, California, with a Ford that swerves into his path in the wrong lane

I N T R O D U C T I O N

*F*airmount, Indiana. A light drizzle hangs in a thin veil of mist over Back Creek cemetery, a mile out of town. In the gathering dusk, a figure can be seen flitting through the graves, rucksack bouncing on its back, guilt written into every step of its flight. Inside that rucksack will be soil stolen from one particular grave, or perhaps a pebble or a blade of grass, or even a chipping of precious pink marble from the headstone. For this is where the vandals and the fans come in equal numbers – not, in their eyes, to desecrate that one special grave, but to pay it their own twisted tribute by stealing a small memento almost half a century after its occupant died too young, tragically and violently.

In their homage they leave their flowers, their messages, their lipstick imprints on the headstone, and their heartfelt pleas for him to come back . . .

A one-line inscription reads simply: *JAMES B.* [for Byron] *DEAN.* It is the third such monument to be erected and systematically eroded – ever since the death at the age of twenty-four of the charismatic young actor who became an icon for millions of teenagers and spawned a legend that exists to this day.

James Dean died at 5.45 p.m. on Friday 30 September 1955, at the intersection of Routes 466 (now 46) and 41 east of Cholame, in the County of San Luis Obispo, California. Minutes earlier, he had been driving his sports car at 130 mph.

ONE

EARLY DAYS

The sign on Highway 26 states proudly: Fairmount – Home of James Dean. And indeed Fairmount, Indiana (population 3,400 and located fifty miles north of Indianapolis), was where James Byron Dean grew up and made his home after being taken there by his parents at the tender age of ten months.

The town itself, just a speck on the map of Indiana, is like many other small Midwest towns in the Bible Belt of America. Main Street boasts a hardware store, the Citizens' Bank, a post office, a library and a single beer hall (closed on Sundays), while East Washington has the Fairmount Historical Museum and the surgery that once belonged to old Doc Holliday, the genial local practitioner who had no relation whatsoever to any nefarious activities that occurred elsewhere at a certain OK Corral in Tombstone, Arizona, in 1881.

Off Main Street you can find the offices of the weekly newspaper the *Fairmount News*, the town hall, the local school and fifteen churches – including the Quaker meeting house where visiting ministers would exhort the locals on the evils of drinking and smoking, and tender advice on living a God-fearing existence – or facing the wrath of the Almighty.

Outside Fairmount, mile upon mile of golden corn stretches away to the horizon, with grain silage towers jutting like sentinels against a landscape of scattered farm buildings and fields where pigs root in acres of muddy grass.

Jimmy, as he was called by all who knew him, had been born ten miles away in Marion, a busy metropolis with a population of fifty thousand. But when Winton and Mildred Dean took their baby son to settle in Fairmount, they were returning to the family base. Fairmount had been founded in the early nineteenth century by Joseph Winslow, one of James Dean's distant ancestors, who with other hardened pioneers had journeyed West in covered wagons through the Cumberland Gap in search of a new life.

The town prospered as a farming community, growing corn and beans on the fertile flat fields, and raising pigs and cattle on the rich pastureland. Around 1900, a group of business-men set up the Fairmount Mining Company to market natural gas, which was indigenous to the area – indeed, Gas City still lies a few miles down the road today, though in Fairmount agriculture would remain the town's chief economic lifeblood.

The other major industry that kept the townsfolk active was religion – strictly the old-time kind. The pioneer founders had been members of the Religious Society of Friends, the Christian sect commonly known as the Quakers, founded in England in 1630 by Robert Fox, who would admonish his flock to 'tremble at the word of the Lord'. Hence their title.

Quakers have no formal creed, ritual or priesthood, refer to their churches as meeting houses, and anyone moved by the Holy Spirit is encouraged to stand up and speak. In the years before the Second World War Fairmount supported two Friends' meeting houses, and little Jimmy Dean attended Back Creek Friends Church – where eventually he would appear in public in his first acting role.

Jimmy was born on 8 February 1931 — just over six months after his parents had taken out a marriage licence at the Grant County Court House in Marion on 26 July 1930. His father Winton Dean was twenty-two, a tall, handsome man who worked as a dental technician at the Veterans' Administration Hospital in Marion. His mother Mildred, just twenty, loved the arts and recited poetry in local churches.

It has been said that James Dean was an unwanted child, and grew up with the stigma of knowing it, in a time when illegitimacy was a social disgrace to both parents and offspring. But Mildred, at least, was devoted to her baby son. Her younger sister Ruth Stegmoller would recall: 'She adored Jimmy. She just loved that little boy.'[1] Winton was more reserved, distant and cold towards the son he never intended should have come into the world so soon, if at all.

They waited for ten months. Then, confident that enough time had passed for people to forget exactly when they were married or the date when little Jimmy had been born, Winton and Mildred moved from their cramped apartment in Marion back to Fairmount. After a brief stay with Winton's parents, they rented a cottage close to Back Creek, which was a small stream that bordered the edge of the farm owned by Winton's brother-in-law Marcus Winslow, surrounded by 180 acres of rich agricultural land.

Times were hard immediately after the Great Depression, and money was tight. Three extra mouths to feed proved too much of a burden, even though Marcus and his wife Ortense were kindly, hard-working people active in community affairs. Winton and Mildred took their small son to West Los Angeles when Winton was offered work in the Sawtelle Veterans' Administration, and the family rented a five-room furnished flat in Santa Monica where Jimmy was enrolled at the local McKinley School. They scraped together enough money to pay for their four-year-old son to take violin and tap dancing lessons, his first brush with show business.

Suddenly, when young Jimmy was nine, his mother began to suffer from severe stomach pains. Her mother Minnie Mae had died from cancer, and now X-rays revealed that Mildred was suffering from cancer of the uterus, already considerably advanced. Winton made the agonising decison to tell his young son that his mother was dying, and would not be with them much longer. 'Jimmy said nothing. He just looked at me,' Winton later recalled. 'Even as a child he wasn't much to speak about things close to him. He never liked to talk about his hurts.'

On 14 July 1940, Mildred Dean died in hospital in Santa Monica at the age of twenty-nine. Jimmy and his father were at her bedside.

GROWING UP

Now came a pivotal period in the formative years of the young James Dean, a time that would leave an indelible mark on his psyche and, indeed, on his whole attitude to life. His father literally abandoned him to his uncle and aunt, sending him back to Fairmount alone on the train from Los Angeles – alone, that is, apart from his mother's coffin in the box-car. Each time the train stopped on its interminable journey across 2,000 miles of mountain and desert, young Jimmy would run down the platform to make sure the coffin was still there.

Back home, Mildred's open casket lay in the Winslow front room for two days – and minutes before her burial Jimmy slipped into the room and snipped off a lock of her hair which he kept under his pillow for months.

His mother's death left him deeply affected and insecure. Two weeks after his return he broke down weeping at his desk during arithmetic class. 'I miss my mother,' he told his teacher tearfully as she comforted him.[1]

He attended West Ward elementary school, where one of his teachers Bertha Seward noted: 'Jimmy wasn't trouble, he wasn't a bad boy. He was more subdued and reserved than the other boys, just a good little kid, although in years to come I think he felt terribly mistreated that he had to lose his mother. I don't believe he ever got over her death.'[2]

Mistreated, resentful even? But at least Uncle Marcus and Aunt Ortense had welcomed him with open arms, and soon Jimmy was calling them Mom and Dad and had settled down in the two-storey white-framed farmhouse built in 1904, with its thirteen rooms and L-shaped wooden porch. They even turned over their own bedroom to little Jimmy, while his aunt encouraged him to sketch, paint and sculpt with clay.

He was an average student, and as he grew older he made waves on the sporting field where he showed particular prowess at basketball, playing for the school team.

Back home in the evenings, Uncle Marcus would give him jobs around the farm, milking, gathering new-laid eggs, feeding the cattle. Marcus turned the barn into a gymnasium, installed a trapeze, and encouraged the lad to work out and keep fit. Indeed, Jimmy was already something of a daredevil — as the daring young man on the home-made flying trapeze he broke four front teeth in one stunt, and it was his father back in Los Angeles who eventually made a dental bridge to repair the damage. Jimmy wore it for the rest of his life.

If he was small for his age, Jimmy was sturdy and agile, though he had to wear glasses because he was short-sighted. By now it had not passed his guardians' notice that he was drawn to the theatre, and exhibited all the signs of being a natural entertainer. Jimmy had a gift for mimicry, and would delight his friends with impromptu and irreverent impressions of neighbours and teachers.

He listened for hours on end to the radio in the Winslows' living-room, and would daydream out loud about 'getting into the movies', causing his new mother and father to smile indulgently at the prospect of an Indiana farm boy taking Hollywood by storm. Even today Fairmount has no cinema — but they screen films at the town hall.

Jimmy was becoming more determined about his wish to act, and finally Ortense asked him to read in a contest held by her local Temperance Union. The boy was only ten, but he stepped up with a confidence beyond his years and won a silver medal. In later readings he would walk away with a gold medal clutched proudly in one small hand.

At Back Creek Church, which he attended with the Winslows every Sunday evening, various groups put on plays, and at the age of twelve Jimmy finally got his wish. He was invited to act in a Christmas play called *To Them that Sleep in Darkness*, portraying a blind boy who regains his vision. His performance was so touching that many in the audience remembered it for years afterwards. One resident recalled: 'Jimmy played a little blind boy who had been healed during the play. At the end, just before the curtain came down, there was a star shining up in the ceiling. You knew he had been healed when he looked up and said: "Mother, look! I can see the star!" It was so moving, it brought tears to our eyes.'[3]

In autumn 1943 Jimmy started the seventh grade, which meant moving to Fairmount High School for his senior studies. On 2 November his aunt gave birth to a son, christened Marcus Junior, nicknamed Markie, and suddenly Jimmy was sharing the family home with a new arrival, though from all accounts he accepted his young cousin as a brother, and they remained friends over the years ahead.

It was at this time that young Jimmy, aged twelve, acquired his first taste for speed. It would develop into an addiction that became the talk of the neighbourhood, whether it was rigging up a ramp in the barn that ran from the hayloft and down to the barn door – where he would whoosh down it on a 'dolly cart' – or pedal a bike at hair-raising pace around the yard and out into the country roads.

Uncle Marcus waited until Jimmy reached the 'right age', and on his nephew's fifteenth birthday bought the young tearaway a Whizzer – a 1.5 hp Czech CZ motorcycle. It lit the touchpaper for a youngster who was to become obsessed with the heady oxygen of the fast lane – Jimmy would delight in performing such stunts as racing along at 50 mph while lying flat on the saddle, face down, and doing 'wheelies' long before such stunts became part of the youth culture that exists today.

His uncle Marcus once said, tellingly, some months after Dean's death crash: 'If Jimmy had fallen just once, things might have been different. But he never got hurt, and he never found anything he couldn't do well almost the first time he tried it. Just one fall off that bike, and maybe he would have been afraid of speed – but he was without fear.'[4]

It was almost inevitable that Jimmy would fall prey to his passion for fast cars. One of his school friends owned a souped-up 1934 Plymouth, complete with a rumble seat, and the boys took turns in driving it. Young daredevil Dean won the respect of his fellow pupils by achieving the record for hurtling through 'Suicide Curve', an S-bend on a gravel road ironically situated close to Back Street cemetery, sliding through the bend at close to 70 mph.

Once, with eerie shades of one of the heart-stopping scenes in *Rebel Without a Cause*, Jimmy was challenged to a race by another boy, driving a Chevy. The other lad tried to keep up, failed, and crashed on the potentially lethal S-bend, rolling the car over and over but luckily emerging unscathed – unlike the rival roadster Buzz who took on Jim Stark (Dean) in the notorious 'chicken run' in the movie, and paid the ultimate price.

At night Jimmy and his pals would pile into the '34 Plymouth and roar off to the Hill Top Drive Inn close to the Marion city limits to drink frosted non-alcoholic beer, listen to the jukebox, and try to catch the eye of the local girls, just like so many other healthy teenagers coming of age in that postwar era that seems so innocent today.

Yet in those formative years in high school, James Dean never had a steady girl-friend, and it is from this time that those pundits who questioned his sexual tendencies in later years started to search for the first clues.

In his mid-teens, Jimmy was more interested in fast cars, bikes, sport, and the arts than in dating, although it is evident that girls found him attractive, and there were numerous 'double dates' when he went out in a foursome with his best friend Clyde Smitson and a chosen couple of local lasses.

More significantly, another kind of relationship began that would confuse the young teenager even more as he tried to come to terms with his emotions. Dr James DeWeerd was minister of the local Wesleyan church in Fairmount, a charismatic man in his thirties who had served as a chaplain with the US Army in the Second World War at Monte

Cassino. He had come home from the field of battle with a Silver Star for gallantry, a Purple Heart, and a deep dent in his stomach from shrapnel wounds.

The good pastor was openly critical of Fairmount and its stultifying atmosphere, and would deliver searing sermons from the pulpit; their passion and zeal riveted his awed parishioners. Unmarried and much-travelled, he lived with his mother, and would lecture his flock on the beauty of literature, art, and poetry. Highly respected in some quarters, in others he was nicknamed Dr Weird, particularly by the groups of boys he would take to the YMCA gymnasium in nearby Anderson, where he would persuade them all to swim nude together.

In the young James Dean, Pastor DeWeerd saw more than just another farm boy. He became Jimmy's mentor, inviting him home to dine with his aged mother, with white linen and silver on the table and the music of Tchaikovsky in the background. Jimmy fell under the spell of his host's charm and eloquence, but all too soon the mutual attraction would descend to an unhealthy level.

One piece of advice the minister gave him stayed with the young would-be actor for life: 'The more things you know how to do and the more things you experience, the better off you will be . . .'[5] It struck a chord, and became the yardstick by which James Dean would measure his life.

The incongruous pair would go for regular spins together in the pastor's convertible Chevrolet through the country lanes and fields, and it was on one of these drives that Dr DeWeerd turned off and parked under a tree. He had seldom talked about his wartime experiences, but now he described how a shell blast had torn a gaping hole in his stomach. He asked Jimmy if he would like to put his hand in the wound, which was as big as the boy's fist. Gingerly, half-fascinated, half-repulsed, Dean did so — and found himself both frightened and excited by the intimate touch as he clenched his fist and placed it in the fleshy crater.

The stories of James Dean's reported bisexuality can be traced back to this one defining moment, in a relationship that was kept secret from the townsfolk of Fairmount and, until much later, from Jimmy's own circle of friends. People noticed, people talked. But in the Bible Belt where tradition and convention were so strictly observed most of them chose to ignore the implications and looked the other way.

The profound influence that Dr DeWeerd had on his young protégé was revealed in a rare interview with columnist and author Joe Hyams, in which the pastor recalled how he had taken Jimmy, then aged sixteen, to a race at the famous Indianapolis circuit. Afterwards they talked about speed, danger and the prospect of sudden death. 'I taught Jimmy to believe in personal immortality,' DeWeerd said. 'He had no fear of death because he believed, as I do, that death is merely control of mind over matter.'[6] That reassuring, if flawed, philosophy may well have affected the thinking of James Dean in the years ahead – until it was too late.

His art teacher Gurney Maddingly recalled Jimmy as a promising student, with one painting in particular branded on his memory – of a line of people emerging from a grave.

Meanwhile, Jimmy pursued his acting ambitions with zest. His mercurial talent needed to be harnessed, and the person who stepped forward to perform this vital function was Adeline Nall, the drama tutor at Fairmount High, who also taught speech, Spanish and English at the college, and sponsored the Thespian Society.

Adeline recognised the raw talent of her new pupil, and a year after he captivated his audience as the blind boy she put him into another school play, the legendary horror tale of *The Monkey's Paw*, in the role of a young man mangled to death in factory machinery after falling foul of a three-wishes curse.

This was followed a year later by *Mooncalf Mugford*, with Jimmy playing an insane elderly man who had visions – and he startled the audience of parents and pupils by practically throttling the poor schoolgirl playing his wife in his enthusiasm for the role.

While still at school, Jimmy featured in four other productions: the comedy *Our Hearts Were Young and Gay* (1947) set in Paris, *Goon With the Wind*, produced for Hallowe'en on 29 October 1948, the gentle satire *You Can't Take it With You* (1949) that had won an Oscar for Frank Capra in 1938 (with James Stewart), and finally *The Madman's Manuscript*.

This last was a reading from Charles Dickens' *Pickwick Papers*, the purported memoirs of a raving lunatic, and Dean won first place at state level in a competition – only to lose out in the national finals because, despite warnings from his tutor, he overran his allotted ten-minute slot by two minutes, and paid the price. When the results were posted on the noticeboard, Jimmy went straight to his desk and huddled in his seat, inconsolable.

But he had learned another lesson – the importance of self-discipline. It was one he would not always obey.

THREE

MAKING WAVES

In the summer of 1949 James Dean headed west with one aim in mind overriding all others: to make a last effort to be reconciled with his father. He was eighteen years old, and up to that point the major influences in his life had been two surrogate father figures — Marcus Winslow and the Revd James DeWeerd. Now it was time to try to come to terms with the past and heal the rift with his genuine parent to help him face an uncertain future.

Winton Dean had remarried, and with his new wife Ethel had moved into a small apartment on Saltair Avenue near the Veterans' Administration Hospital, Los Angeles, where he was still working in the dental clinic. He had rarely written to his son, and sent only sporadic cheques to the Winslows for Jimmy's upkeep. But Jimmy had enjoyed his teenage years, filled with the genuine affection of his uncle and aunt, home comforts, and a degree of moral training.

Educationally, his grades were only average —
mostly D — but after discussions with his Fairmount
tutors it was decided that Jimmy would enrol at
Santa Monica City College for a semester (a fifteen-
week term, part of the US academic year) to see
how he developed.

Winton met him at Los Angeles station, and
found his son had grown into a young man with a
steady, challenging blue gaze and a mind of his own.
All Jimmy's worldly possessions were in a single
battered brown suitcase, but after an initial rather
stilted embrace and handshake in the arrival hall he
refused to call Winston 'Dad', opting instead for the
more formal 'Father'. From the outset, the boy
found himself at odds with both his father and
stepmother over his future. Ethel was by all
accounts a domineering woman who resented the
sudden reappearance of the son from her husband's
first marriage, while Winton wanted something
more stable for him than acting.

On the surface, Winton tried hard, and that is
where the relationship stayed, with no real depth of
feeling evident in Jimmy's early weeks under a new
roof. Despite his protestations that he wanted to
tread the boards and face the cameras, his father had

in mind a safer career, such as a PE teacher or, better still, a lawyer. Since his father was paying the bills, Jimmy acquiesced, enrolling at the City College as a pre-law student in January 1950; in return Winton bought him a 1939 Chevrolet sedan so that he could drive there each day.

Against his father's wishes, Jimmy signed up for all the available theatre classes, involving everything from acting to set designing and shifting scenery. He also joined a local theatre group in Los Angeles, and revealed his excitement in a triumphant letter to his 'real Mom and Dad' back in Fairmount, telling Marcus and Ortense how he was now a fully fledged member of the Miller Playhouse Theatre Group, and that his knowledge of the stage and ability to design and paint sets had won him the position of head stage manager.

James Dean would not stay out of the spotlight for long. As well as painting the scenery, he also featured in a small role in the Playhouse summer stock production of a California gold rush spoof called *The Romance of Scarlet Gulch* – in which he was billed under the name of Byron James and played a drunk. He was also given minor parts in *She Was Only a Farmer's Daughter* (melodrama) and *Iz Zat So?* (comedy revue).

Now Dean pressed on with the single-minded determination, amounting to tunnel vision, that he would exhibit throughout his short but eventful life. His faith in himself paid off when Gene Owen, head of the City College drama department, found Jimmy sitting in the front row of her radio class.

She asked him to read scenes from Edgar Allan Poe's *The Telltale Heart* — and her verdict was: 'Magnificent!' Afterwards she began to give the eager, intense young student private tuition in the evenings, putting him through hour-long 'oral interpretations' of *Hamlet*, and later recalling: 'Jimmy had some problems with articulation, but I told him that if anything would clear up fuzzy speech it would be the demanding soliloquies of Shakespeare. He would read alone, and memorise all the soliloquies. If Jimmy could have done Hamlet on Broadway some day, it would have been a revolutionary role.'[1]

Gene's enthusiasm led to her hiring her young protégé as an announcer on the college FM radio station. He also found time to play for the basketball team, become a member of the Jazz Appreciation Club, and hang out with friends at Ray Avery's Record Roundup store down the road, listening to the latest releases. At the end of his term, he brought home A grades in drama and gymnastics – and a lowly C in pre-law. Faced with this evidence of where his son's true vocation lay, Winton reluctantly agreed that he could enrol at UCLA, the University of California, Los Angeles, to study theatre arts.

Before starting the autumn term Jimmy worked through the summer vacation in a variety of part-time jobs, mainly to earn a few extra dollars. One of his jobs was as an usher at a Santa Monica cinema at night, while by day he was an athletics intructor at a boys' camp in the suburb of Glendora.

University life began – but at home tensions had simmered and finally boiled over. Young Dean could no longer stand the atmosphere in the apartment, and there were heated, bitter arguments and confrontations that made life impossible for the would-be thespian.

By a fortunate coincidence Winton and Ethel chose that month to move house to another Los Angeles suburb, Reseda, giving Jimmy the chance to break away from his father and move on to campus at UCLA. He was allocated a room in a fraternity house on Gayley Avenue, but from the beginning it was apparent he would have difficulty settling in to the give-and-take of campus life.

He stayed aloof from in-house activities and spent much of his time in his room, painting bizarre sketches – one was a bloodshot eyeball suspended in mid-air staring at a blackened forest.

Jimmy lasted there a month, and found himself the object of some derision from his macho fellow-students who poked fun at the country lad in the blue jeans with his Indiana twang, called him 'hick' or 'plough-boy', and finally crossed the Rubicon when one of them called him a 'fruit' to his face.

Jimmy, his temper always on a short fuse, exploded. He clenched his fists and leaped on his tormentor, swinging punches furiously. By the time the pair were separated the other boy was flat on his back, bruised and scared. The brawl reached the ears of the head tutor, and Dean was ordered to leave. He walked out, leaving behind an unpaid bill of $45.

But he had also made friends, and one of them, fellow acting student Bill Bast, was in similar dire lodging straits. They decided to share an apartment, and found a three-room Mexican-style flat in Santa Monica, complete with a high beamed ceiling, Aztec furniture, and a breathtaking view of the Pacific from the balcony, which was reached by an outside set of stairs covered with fronds hanging from a palm tree. They christened it 'The Penthouse', and even though the rent was a painful $300 a month, both young men knew it was the place where they could take on the world.

Jimmy described his feelings to Bill in one evocative outburst: 'I want to grow so tall that nobody can reach me. Not to prove anything, but just to go where you ought to go when you devote your whole life and all you are to one thing.'[2] The Penthouse was a good place to start the crusade.

Now came another pivotal role in James Dean's career: in October the UCLA theatre department announced a major production of *Macbeth* to be staged in their showcase Royce Hall. Jimmy auditioned – and beat 360 other hopefuls to become a member of the cast, with his name on the programme in the key role of Malcolm.

The play ran from 29 November to 2 December, and afterwards the reviews, to put it kindly, were mixed. One observer remarked on Dean's 'energy and inventiveness', while another dismissed his opening-night performance as akin to 'an agonising dental extraction'. This sentiment was echoed by the UCLA newsletter *Spotlight* which reported that James Dean's portrayal of Malcolm 'failed to show any growth, and would have made him a hollow king'. Jimmy, nursing his bruised ego, was man enough to admit his shortcomings and improved considerably over the next three nights. The tutoring he had received from Gene Owen had helped him overcome any fears of Shakespeare's language, and indeed he seemed to revel in his new-found oratory.

The legacy left to Dean by *Macbeth* was not the reviews to be mulled over, or the opinions of his fellow students, but the presence in the first-night audience of a woman named Isabelle Draesemer. She was a highly respected agent, wealthy and independent enough to own her own company, and after watching the young unknown she felt sufficiently impressed to offer to put him on her books. Jimmy accepted with alacrity. The UCLA theatre productions in Westwood were a regular target for talent agencies – but it was unusual for an untrained student to land an agent on the first night of his first show.

Isabelle moved fast. Within days she found her young client his first paid job as an actor, in a Pepsi-

Cola television commercial. It was filmed in Griffith Park on 13 December 1950, and the final version lasted two minutes.

In the first scene Jimmy dances around a juke-box with a group of typical all-American teenagers. In the second he wears a sailor suit and sings 'Live it up with Pepsi-Cola' as he hands out the drinks to the other youngsters whirling past him on a carousel. For one day's work he received a flat fee of $25 — and a free lunch.

Interestingly, two of the other unknowns in that commercial would have roles in *Rebel Without a Cause* four years later — Beverly Long (playing Helen) and Nick Adams (Moose). And it was Nick who would be called on to deliver James Dean's valedictory speech in *Giant* — posthumously.

As happens so often in show business, one opportunity leads to another, and days later the phone rang in Isabelle's office in Beverly Hills. The commercial's producer Jerry Fairbanks had been so impressed with Jimmy's brief but telling appearance that he wanted him to audition for an Easter TV special called *Hill Number One*, an hour-long religious drama that would reach an estimated forty-two million viewers. It was an allegorical tale set in the Korean War, opening with a group of disenchanted American GIs questioning why they are bombarding a particular hill.

An army chaplain arrives with coffee for the men, and attempts to lift their morale. 'War is a crucifixion,' he intones. 'It shakes the earth, darkens the sun and makes men look for a meaning in life.' Then he tells them the story of a man who had taken one hill all on his own – a hill called Calvary. The story of the Crucifixion and Resurrection is then told in flashback, with Joseph of Arimathea and Pontius Pilate discussing what to do with the corpse of Jesus Christ.

The massed cast of fifty included names who would go on to greater things, headed by Leif Erickson (Pilate), Roddy McDowall, Henry Brandon, Joan Leslie, Ruth Hussey and Gene Lockhart.

James Dean, with curly hair and clean-shaven, had only two scenes in his role as John the Apostle, for which he wore a *jellaba* and sat at a table with other disciples who are discussing the prospect of disbanding. He rebukes them: 'Was it for this that we gave up our nets – just to go back to our boats again?'

His was a minor part, but it was prime time television, and one area that Jimmy won over was the Immaculate Heart School in Los Angeles, where *Hill Number One* had been required viewing. The young ladies were so moved by the 'sincerity and spirituality' of his performance that they formed the first known James Dean Fan Club. As for the object of their affections, he had disguised the fact that he was suffering both from nerves and laryngitis — which made his voice deeper than usual — and walked off with the impressive fee of $150. At least he could pay the rent for another month.

Money and James Dean were never bosom buddies, and in those early days the young actor was broke for much of the time. In common with struggling actors the world over, Jimmy and Bill lived life on a shoestring, often behind with the rent but somehow able to bluff and cajole their way through, picking up cash wherever they could. Bill spent his spare hours writing scripts, all of which were rejected, earning pocket-money from working after school hours in the radio workshop at CBS, and finding a job there for Jimmy as a car park attendant on the studio lot.

On the personal side, it has been alleged that Jimmy was drawn to Bill both emotionally and physically, but there has never been more than speculation on this score. In fact one thing the pair had in common was their attraction to the opposite sex, and they used Jimmy's '39 Chevy to go out in foursomes, or double-dating as it was known.

It was some time later that Jimmy was drawn into the notorious, largely unknown, homosexual network that provided a secret subculture to the Hollywood of the fifties.

FOUR

ONWARD AND UPWARD

Parking cars can have its advantages, especially if you are working in a film or broadcasting studio, as James Dean found out one day at the CBS car park on Sunset Boulevard, when he took the wheel from an advertising executive named Rogers Brackett, who worked for a prestige New York agency named Foote, Cone and Belding. The year was 1951, a time when advertising agencies played a crucial role in the creative side of radio and TV production. Many programmes were funded and produced by these agencies, from the script to the casting and on to the eventual recording of the show – complete, of course, with the obligatory plug for a product.

Brackett was a homosexual, and took an instant shine to Jimmy, with his sensitive features and muscular body. The attraction was mutual. Jimmy had quarrelled with Bill Bast – ironically over a girlfriend whom Bill had accused him of 'stealing'. Now the young actor moved out of The Penthouse, and into a luxury apartment with the wealthy and influential advertising man.

Successful and with connections in high places, the 35-year-old Rogers became a pivotal figure in Jimmy's burgeoning future. The tall, suavely handsome executive knew all the right people to further his young live-in companion's career. One of his accounts was the weekly radio show *Alias Jane Doe*, and Jimmy found himself in a minor role within days of moving in with his new mentor, who also happened to be the director. Two more shows followed in rapid succession: *Hallmark Playhouse* and *Stars Over Hollywood*.

Soon after this, he was given a small part in his first feature film. *Sailor Beware* was an early Dean Martin–Jerry Lewis comedy, with Jerry up to his usual tricks as a moronic, cross-eyed, frenetic clown endeavouring to plant a kiss on the cheek of shapely French siren Corinne Calvet. Martin and Lewis were already phenomenally successful, even if one critic had described them as the unfunniest couple since Burke and Hare, but for Jimmy it was a major breakthrough. He set foot on the Paramount lot under the eye of a top producer, the legendary Hal Wallis, and he was even given a small speaking part. Cast as a second in a spoof boxing match in the corner of Jerry Lewis's opponent, he tied on the gloves, flapped the towel, massaged his man's shoulders, and uttered the immortal line: 'That guy's a professional.'

More work followed through the influence of Rogers Brackett. That same year the agent persuaded his friend Samuel Fuller — a controversial director and one-time crime reporter whose unique visual style had given him a huge cult following — to hire Dean for *Fixed Bayonets*, a war movie set in Korea but filmed entirely within the confines of the 20th Century-Fox studios.

It was a psychological drama starring Richard Basehart as a corporal assuming a command he did not want, and facing life or death decisions. Jimmy appeared at the end as a sentry, with another one-liner: 'I think I hear them coming!' Not exactly earth-shattering, and since he wore a helmet with his face blackened, and the sequence was shot at night, he was hardly likely to stand out in a crowd.

But he was moving around the studios. Paramount . . . Fox . . . and now, with *Has Anybody Seen My Gal?* Jimmy set foot on the sprawling sets at Universal. This would become an ironic situation for the trio of major Hollywood studios to mull over later, since the only three films for which James Dean would be remembered would be backed by Warner Bros. The other three all had him under their roof – and they all lost him. But . . . that's show business.

Dean was content with a ten-second appearance in this lightweight comedy set in the 1920s with some heavyweight muscle, led by Rock Hudson who was then climbing the middle rungs of a career that would eventually bring him together on the screen with Jimmy in the epic *Giant*.

Veteran Charles Coburn played an eccentric millionaire who disguises himself as a pauper to see if a family to whom he planned to leave his fortune would spend it wisely. He even takes on a job as a waiter in an ice-cream parlour, even though he could have bought the place ten times over.

Dean was cast as a laid-back college boy ordering an ice-cream sundae, and the dialogue went like this:

Dean:	Hey, gramps! I'll have a choc malt, heavy on the choc, plenty of milk, four spoons of malt, two scoops of vanilla ice cream, one floating.
Coburn:	Would you like to come in on Wednesday for a fitting?

The critics gave the film a thumbs-up, and so did the public. Most of them were there for 'the Rock', because Rock Hudson was amassing his own following. What was kept secret at that time, hidden in Hollywood's dark corridors and closets of power, was the homosexual subculture within the artistic community.

Jimmy had become Rogers Brackett's lover. Brackett knew another well-known agent, Henry Willson, who represented many gay actors (although use of that adjective had yet to find its way into the patois), among them Rock Hudson. Willson's parties were legendary for the 'closet community', and Jimmy became a well-known figure in that undercover circle.

But despite the poolside parties and the gossip and the in-crowd of movers and shakers, Jimmy could not shake off a nagging frustration. He had so much to give, and so little was on offer. He was not fulfilling himself – and, as happens, he was falling out with his mentor in frequent rows over a lifestyle that was looking emptier by the day.

Finally he heard of an actor called James Whitmore, a solid, grizzled ex-Marine who had made his mark playing tough characters in key secondary roles, one of which earned him an Oscar nomination for best supporting actor in the 1949 war film *Battleground*. Whitmore ran a small informal group of actors who met once a week in a rehearsal room off San Vicente Boulevard. The idea appealed to Jimmy, and he joined the classes.

In the second week he approached his tutor with the due respect accorded to a screen veteran who exuded authority and experience, and came to the point without preamble. 'Mr Whitmore,' he said. 'How do you get to be an actor?'

'There's only one way, Jimmy,' the big man answered. 'Stop dissipating your energy and talent. Go to New York. There you will find out whether you can take the uncertainty of an actor's life. Give it the total effort, and don't do it half way. Above all, act! You get to be an actor by acting.'

After a long pause, Jimmy asked: 'Where's the best place to learn?'

'Go see Elia Kazan at the Actors Studio. I don't know if they'll take you, but you can't do any better.'[1]

Jimmy took the words to heart. He resigned from UCLA, and his friend Rogers Brackett drove him to Chicago where the director had business to attend to, before paying the bus fare for Jimmy to go on alone to New York and a future full of hope but fraught with uncertainty.

James Dean arrived in New York in early September 1951, with less than $150 in his pocket. But he had letters of introduction, and moved into the Iroquois Hotel close to Times Square, where he rented a small room for his first weeks in the Big Apple.

Coming to terms with the hustle and bustle of New York proved harder than he had anticipated, and in his first letter home to his Uncle Marcus and his 'Mom' Ortense, he poured his heart out.

He revealed how he saw three films a day in an attempt to escape from his loneliness and depression, and spent most of his limited funds just seeing movies. He sat through Marlon Brando's

The Men four times in two days, and saw *A Place in the Sun*, starring that other Method actor Montgomery Clift, three times.

In those heady days, New York was the hub of TV production, with more than thirty live shows put out each week. Aspiring actors would queue for mass auditions known as 'cattle calls', and Jimmy found himself just a face in the crowd of up to a thousand other wannabes filing past producers and casting directors in the hope that they would stand out.

Names that would later blaze out in neon lights from the front of cinemas across the world clustered in groups of ten to be given a number and called up on stage for a few nerve-racking seconds before departing into the wings and out on to the cold, impersonal streets. Names like Paul Newman, Steve McQueen, John Cassavetes, Ben Gazzara, Tony Franciosa, Martin Landau, were among the hopefuls. James Dean got to know them all, and they in turn grew to recognise the moody, introspective kid who was already showing the rebellious traits that would stamp his place in screen history.

After two months on this soul-destroying treadmill, Dean was finally hired for a job that was hardly designed to test his acting skills – on the popular TV game show *Beat the Clock*, hosted by Bob Collyer. Members of the audience were invited up to perform silly and usually messy stunts within a time limit, usually a minute; this long-running show later made its mark in the UK, with Bruce Forsyth as its indefatigably cheerful host.

In New York unemployed actors were engaged at $5 an hour to try out the stunts backstage and make sure they were safe. Jimmy, taken on more for his athletic prowess than his looks or ability, took each game as a personal challenge, and refused to give up until he had triumphed – even after the show was long over, and in his own time.

Invariably broke, Jimmy moved from lodging to lodging, shacking up with sympathetic acting friends who would give him a bed for a night, or a week. They would discover, to their surprise and amusement, that their young guest never ate chicken or eggs – he had grown up on a farm, he said, and could not stand the sight or the taste of either.

Romance came briefly into his life in 1952 when he met a tall, sensuous dance student named Elizabeth Sheridan (known as Dizzy) at a club frequented by young artists, and found an instant mutual attraction. She told friends later: 'When we met I was ready to be involved, and I guess Jimmy was too. He seemed very lost, which I found attractive. He took me to Jerry's Bar on Sixth Avenue, we sat in a booth, and we sort of fell in love just talking across the table.'[2]

They moved into a room in an unpretentious hotel off Columbus Avenue, but after only a few weeks Rogers Brackett appeared in New York, and tempted Jimmy with the invitation to move in with him into his luxury apartment off Broadway, rent free, meeting the wheeler-dealers of show-business. Jimmy accepted, and Dizzy took the blow surprisingly well, remarking only: 'Jimmy was confused about his sexuality. I guess it was time for us to separate, but we still stayed friends.'[3]

Back in elite company, James Dean found himself rubbing shoulders at parties with the likes of Grace Kelly, Maureen Stapleton, Tennessee Williams, Maggie McNamara, and Sir Winston Churchill's actress daughter Sarah. Within two weeks he had landed another TV role, playing a vagrant in a murder mystery entitled *Sleeping Dogs* for CBS, and the following month he was cast in two more dramas for the same network: *Ten Thousand Horses Singing* and *The Foggy, Foggy Dew*. During that year his roles varied from a bellhop to a foster child, from a soldier to an aristocrat, and even an angel standing at the Pearly Gates.

But it was on 12 November 1952 that James Dean reached and passed a milestone in his career: he auditioned before Elia Kazan, artistic director Lee Strasberg, and the panel of judges at the Actors Studio.

Some weeks previously he had met a young blonde receptionist named Christine White at an agency, and began chatting to her. It turned out that this was her day job – she was an out-of-work actress and would-be scriptwriter, and was busy writing a sketch that she planned to perform herself at the Actors Studio.

The theme revolved around a young couple who meet on an isolated beach at a crucial time in both their lives. Jimmy was intrigued, asked if he could play the male part, and suggested a new title: *Roots*, which came from his usual response to the question: 'What have you been doing for most of your life?' Answer: 'Ripping off layers to find the roots!'[4]

They worked on the scene together for five weeks, rehearsing in buses and taxis, on street corners and on the roof of her apartment building 'to feel the open air'. When the great day dawned, Dean was almost speechless with nerves. Like the other hopefuls, they were allowed five minutes — but the scene ran past the allotted time, for all of fourteen minutes. When it was over, Kazan broke the silence. 'Very nice,' he said. And repeated it. 'Very nice.'[5] They were in!

FIVE

THE ACTORS STUDIO

L ess than a week after his audition, Dean was invited to join the Actors Studio. At twenty-one, he was the youngest member in their history to be offered a place, and overjoyed he wrote home to Marcus and Ortense in Fairmount: 'I have made great strides in my craft. After months of auditioning, I am very proud to announce that I am a member of the Actors Studio, the greatest school of the theatre.'[1]

He reeled off a list of names that he could now count as his fellow thespians, who would now take him seriously: Marlon Brando, Julie Harris, Montgomery Clift, Arthur Kennedy, June Havoc, Roddy McDowall, Kevin McCarthy, Rod Steiger . . . and added: 'Very few get into this school, and it is absolutely free. It is the best thing that can happen to an actor. If I can keep this up, one of these days

I might be able to contribute something to the world.'

His first solo performance in front of Kazan and Strasberg was a monologue from the novel *Matador*, by Barnaby Conrad, tracing the thoughts of a matador preparing for his last bullfight. Jimmy rewrote it himself, but from the moment he began he sensed there was something wrong – with his portrayal, with his delivery, with the material itself.

At the end when he took his seat, Strasberg stood up and gave him a roasting, launching into an acerbic critique of virtually every area of the newcomer's efforts. His attack was so vicious that Kazan remembered the effect on the young actor in his introduction to the Method School: 'Jimmy sat in a sort of poutish mess in the front row, and scowled. Finally he threw his bullfighter's cape over his shoulder, and stalked out.'[2] It was a harsh lesson, and it left a chip on Dean's shoulder for months before he finally came to terms with it.

Originally he and Christine had intended to present a short play they had written together entitled *Abroad*, a duologue between two people planning a trip to Europe. But other members of the ensemble reminded them that this was an actors' studio, not a writers' workshop – lesson two for the young entrant.

Others noted the effect that first flaying had on James Dean. 'He was suffering. It was as if his skin was being pulled off,' said one. But another pointed out: 'Lee [Strasberg] was tough – if you were talented. He could tolerate mediocrity. But if you had talent, he was wicked! He wanted to pull out of you all he knew was there, and he stood no nonsense.'[3]

So the criticism became a compliment, and once Jimmy realised it he was on his way, though his relationship with the fiery artistic director was always volatile. James Dean's relationship with the Method also became a love–hate affair. He wanted to be aware of his performance every moment he was on stage or in front of the cameras.

The Method demanded 'sense, memory and motivation', living each second of the part as if it was actually happening. In these formative months in New York he expanded his interests into music, dance and literature, taking dance lessons from Katherine Dunham, pounding away at a set of bongo drums in the corner of his hotel room, and studying the piano under a professional tutor.

But under the prestigious umbrella of the Actors Studio, James Dean came alive. His range expanded with every new play, starting with *End as a Man*, a harsh essay on life in a military academy with Ben Gazzara playing a sadistic sergeant and Jimmy cast as a cadet officer. This was followed by roles in Chekhov's *The Seagull*, a poetic anti-war play *Aria Da Capo* and a satire on superstition and witchcraft entitled *The Scarecrow*, in which he found himself in the company of such future luminaries as Eli Wallach, Patricia Neal and Bradford Dillman.

Another milestone was reached on 3 December 1952, when Dean opened at the Curt Theatre on Broadway in a play called *See the Jaguar*. He had been offered the part through a friend of Rogers Brackett, one Lemuel Ayers, a big-time theatrical producer who spotted the potential in the moody young actor he had been meeting at Brackett's notorious parties.

The play was described as 'an allegorical Western without a horse'. Make of that what you will, but the story centres around one Wally Wilkins, a guileless teenager whose mother had kept him locked up in a wooden cage since childhood to protect him from the wicked ways of the world.

Jazz-loving James Dean proved
himself a wow on the bongos, as
well as being adept at other
musical instruments.
(© *Dennis Stock / Magnum Photos*)

Giant, Edna Ferber's sprawling saga of cattle barons and oil wells, became an
instant best-seller in 1952, and would sell over 25 million copies in five years.
James Dean won his second Oscar nomination for his performance as Jett
Rink, the farmhand who struck it rich. Here the author is pictured with two
of the film's stars, Rock Hudson and Elizabeth Taylor. (© *Popperfoto*)

James Dean (centre front, wearing spectacles) at the age of fourteen poses with the baseball team of Fairmount High School. An accomplished athlete, Jimmy also played basketball for his school.

(© Rex Features)

Sultry Sicilian-born actress Pier Angeli was chosen to become an 'item' with
James Dean to reinforce the star's image as virile, macho – and heterosexual.
What nobody visualised was that the two would actually fall in love.

(© Rex Features)

Natalie Wood was a doe-eyed beauty of seventeen when she won the coveted leading role opposite James Dean in *Rebel Without a Cause*. She also won an Oscar nomination for her startling performance as Judy, a teenager flowering into womanhood, but with an over-protective father to contend with at home.

(© *Rex Features*)

Ursula Andress was another up-and-coming beauty pictured out on the town with James Dean, with stories of their 'close relationship' circulated for the gossip columns. Seven years later the Swiss actress would make her own big international impact in the first James Bond thriller *Dr No*.
(© *Hulton Getty Picture Collection*)

An early taste for speed. James Dean was given his first motorbike by his
Uncle Marcus at fifteen — and idolised his hero Marlon Brando in the biker
film *The Wild One*.

(© Rex Features)

Not an Oscar, but a trophy that meant as much to speed-crazy James Dean
as any film award. At the wheel he is presented with a prize for winning his
event in a racing car competition in California.

(© Rex Features)

The end of the road. The mangled remains of the silver-grey Porsche
Spyder 550, which James Dean had been driving at more than 100mph.
The date: 30 September 1955. Today his fans still embark on the bizarre
'James Dean Death Drive' in memory of their hero.

(© Rex Features)

Waves of hysteria followed James Dean's death. His headstone in Back
Creek Cemetery is regularly vandalised with fans chipping pieces off it for
souvenirs – and leaving lipstick kisses to mark their abiding homage.

(© Rex Features)

Just before her death, she releases him, leaving him to prowl the mountains with his eyes opened to a new world full of beauty and brutality.

The part seemed tailor-made for Jimmy, and he gave it everything he had – only to see the play fold after five days, despite critical acclaim like the review from the *New York Morning Telegraph*: 'James Dean, making his Broadway stage debut, is overwhelming as the boy brought into a world incomprehensible to him.' The *New York Post*'s critic wrote: 'James Dean achieves the feat of making the childish young fugitive believable and unembarrassing.'

That year, 1953, and the next proved busy ones. Now Jimmy was in the swim, and becoming a bigger fish by the minute.

On the strength of the *Jaguar* reviews, Dean featured in no fewer than seventeen TV productions, specialising in psychotic, tormented youths. In the popular NBC series *Treasury Men in Action* he played a delinquent on the run from federal agents, while in a drama called *The Dark, Dark Hour* he found himself waving a gun in the face of Ronald Reagan (playing a small-town doctor) to force the physician to take care of a wounded accomplice (Jack Simmons, who would later feature in Jimmy's personal life).

But he was also acquiring a reputation for being 'difficult'. Disputes with directors became more frequent as Jimmy became more confident – some would say downright cocky – and wanted to do it his way. The short fuse seemed to be getting shorter by the day. One example of his audacity and lack of regard for his elders came when he was rehearsing for another major breakthrough in *The Immoralist*, a play destined for Broadway and directed by the highly respected Herman Shumlin, a noted theatrical figure.

The theme, sensitive in those days, was homosexuality, with an archaeologist (played by Louis Jourdan) and his alcoholic wife (Geraldine Page) on honeymoon in Africa, only to fall under the spell of their houseboy named Bachir (James Dean in brown make-up and wearing a kaftan) who brings into the open the groom's latent gay feelings.

As each actor read his or her lines, Shumlin would call out: 'No, no!' and then proceed to correct them. When he got to Jimmy, there was a long silence before the young actor finally enquired coldly: 'Mr Shumlin, why are you insulting my intelligence?'[4] The resulting exchange of words brought gulps of disbelief from the watching cast at the way the young upstart was sticking to his guns — and winning through, when the director finally backed down and allowed him to play it his way.

The play opened on Broadway on 8 February 1954 to a standing ovation, but Dean had to make his own gesture by curtseying in his kaftan to the predominantly gay audience, to the fury of the producers. After angry words backstage, Jimmy responded in typical rebellious fashion: by handing in his notice. Two weeks later, he was out of the show.

But someone had been in the audience on that heady first night, someone important. Paul Osborn was a 53-year-old playwright who would later write screenplays for hits like *The World of Suzie Wong*, *Sayonara* and *South Pacific*. At the time he was working on a script for *East of Eden*, and next day he called Elia Kazan to alert him to the dynamic talent he had just witnessed. Remembering the young actor who had once auditioned for him, Kazan agreed to see the play, and immediately realised he had found the actor he wanted to play the crucial role of Cal Trask in his forthcoming film based on John Steinbeck's most ambitious novel since *The Grapes of Wrath*.

The story was a torrid saga spanning half a century, beginning in Monterey in 1917, charting the lives of two farming families, with Cal Trask the wild adolescent rebelling against a stern father and believing his mother dead. Fiction stranger than truth for James Dean? The role would fit him like a glove, with symbolic overtones of his own life — until the mother was found running a nearby brothel, which was never in Dean's personal script. Meanwhile, he had to earn his pay packet.

Kazan (Elia Kazanjoglou, born in Istanbul) had an ingrained skill for spotting maverick talent. He had directed Marlon Brando in the 1947 stage production of *A Streetcar Named Desire*, adapted it into a controversial 1951 film (which won three Academy Awards and starred Vivien Leigh), and gone on to win his own Oscar for *On the Waterfront* in 1954.

He had already considered three of his Method actors for the role: Brando, Paul Newman and Montgomery Clift. But he followed a hunch that James Dean would make the role of Cal come alive — and he would be proved right.

Jimmy, however, being Jimmy, had to behave as if he could take it or leave it. He turned up for his interview with Kazan at the Warner Bros offices in New York in jeans and bomber jacket, and after initial verbal fencing suddenly asked the director: 'How would you like a ride on my bike?'

Recognising the challenge, Kazan agreed. At the end of a palm-moistening race around the traffic-snarled streets of Manhattan, the director recovered sufficiently to call both Osborn and John Steinbeck to tell them he had found the actor to play Cal. He even sent Jimmy over to meet Steinbeck face to face, after which the author called Kazan with the message: 'I think he's a snotty kid!'

'That's irrelevant,' Kazan told him. 'He is Cal, isn't he?'

'He sure as hell is,'[5] the great man agreed. The die was cast — and so was James Dean, in the role that would win him international acclaim in his first film, and win him an Oscar nomination besides.

Jimmy took the call confirming the deal in the tiny one-room apartment he was now renting on West 68th Street, having bade a not unfriendly farewell to his mentor Rogers Brackett before deciding to go it alone. His first reaction was to phone Christine White, his kindred acting spirit. 'Christ!' he shouted. 'I've got it! Chris, come over here right away!'[6]

She later recalled how the room was a mess, with a double bed piled high with dirty washing, the floor and shelves awash with the detritus of bachelor living: a half-full jar of peanut butter, sheet music for his bongo drums, bullfight posters, books of his sketches, a flute, and a copy of *East of Eden*.

Christine looked around, and her opening remark, laughing and crying at the same time to share his triumph, said it all: 'What is Hollywood going to do with you? You've still got hayseed in your hair from Indiana!'[7]

SIX

EAST OF EDEN

In his one-room studio at 19 West 68th Street, James Dean would show friends photographs of his idol: Marlon Brando. They had never met, not yet, but they would do so on the set of Jimmy's forthcoming *East of Eden*. Pride of place in the collection he had amassed was a shot of Brando posing in front of a porthole window, similar to the single window in Jimmy's apartment. Sure enough, the young actor confirmed to his visitors: 'Marlon Brando rented this room.'

But for now he was on a one-way trip west, flying first-class, his ticket paid for by Warner Bros, heading for Los Angeles, Hollywood, and the Boulevard of Broken Dreams that he was about to conquer.

In the next seat sat Elia Kazan, the man who was banking his belief and his reputation on the unknown young actor he had pulled out from the stage of the Actors Studio to face the searing arc lights of a big-time movie studio. Kazan was riding high on a track record that had made him the most bankable director in the business, and studio boss Jack L. Warner authorised an unlimited budget (it would finally work out at £1 million), casting approval, and even control over the final edit of *East of Eden*.

But Kazan knew he had to deliver. He told his paymasters: 'James Dean looked and spoke like the character in the film. When he walked into my office, I knew at once that he was right for the role. He was guarded, sullen, suspicious, and he had a great deal of concealed emotion — which was just what I was looking for.'[1]

From the outset, the shrewd director realised that the thin-skinned young actor he had acquired would be living a role very close to his own life, and that he, Kazan, would have to tread carefully — with a pot of gold waiting at the end of the rainbow if he could make Jimmy bare his innermost feelings to the public gaze. He was playing with dynamite, and an explosion could destroy the whole elaborate charade. But Kazan took his chances.

Firstly, Jimmy had to get a sun-tan. His character Cal Trask was a fit farm boy, not a pale washed-out New York city-dweller. Kazan gave him a week, and ordered him to go into the desert, lie in the sun, 'And drink a pint of cream a day. I want you to gain a few pounds!'[2] Jimmy located his old friend Bill Bast, and they headed off together for Palm Springs. It was at this time, as they sped through the arid brown scrub, that Jimmy first uttered the phrase that would linger long after his death and become his epitaph in the minds of millions: 'Live fast, die young, have a beautiful corpse!'

But right now he was living fast. On 7 April 1954, safely back in Los Angeles, he signed a contract with Warner Bros, while his new agent, Dick Clayton from Famous Artists, hovered protectively at his elbow, reading the small print. To start with he would be earning a thousand dollars a week – not bad in the early 1950s – and he immediately put the money down on a zippy red MG, the first of four sports cars he would buy before he finally ran out of road.

After much wrangling behind the scenes, Kazan and his screenwriter Paul Osborn agreed to base the movie on the last quarter of Steinbeck's rambling novel, a clever move since it accentuated the personal rivalry between the two brothers, Aaron and Cal, for their father's affections.

Steinbeck himself summed up the theme, and it had searing personal overtones for the actor chosen for the seminal role of Cal: 'The greatest terror a child can have is that he is not loved, and rejection is the hell he fears. I think everyone in the world to a large or small extent has felt rejection. And with rejection comes anger . . .'

Kazan tested Joanne Woodward for Abra, the girl both brothers desire, then decided on Julie Harris, an exciting, red-haired actress from his Actors Studio. He tested Paul Newman for the other brother, but chose an unknown named Richard Davalos, who bore a resemblance to Dean.

For the pivotal part of the father he considered Gary Cooper, then selected Raymond Massey, a veteran actor he knew would strike sparks off Jimmy because of his sombre, paternalistic manner, reminiscent of Dean's own father.

Kazan knew his man. 'I chose him because he *was* Cal Trask,' he would reveal later. 'There was no point in attempting to cast it better or nicer. Jimmy was it. He had a grudge against all fathers. He was vengeful. He had a sense of aloneness and of being persecuted. In addition,' he added, almost as an afterthought, 'he was tremendously talented.'[3]

But even the experienced Kazan needed all the patience he could muster when shooting started on location in a small California town called Mendocino, the town that served as Monterey in the film, because in his first featured movie role the young discovery betrayed all the signs of a prima donna. Jimmy worked on pure instinct. He held up shooting every day, causing cast and crew to chafe visibly, because he felt he needed time to prepare fully for the scene ahead. So the others waited . . . and waited . . . and when Dean refused to do a scene the same way twice, an exasperated Raymond Massey finally exploded: 'Make him say the lines the way they're written!'[4]

Finally they moved to the Warner studios at Burbank, which was the moment that James Dean achieved his own dream-come-true. He met his idol Marlon Brando when the magnetic star was invited to the set by Kazan, who had directed him in *On the Waterfront*.

Brando himself has described his first meeting with the moody young lion who in many ways had modelled himself on Marlon's leather-clad anti-hero biker in *The Wild One*: 'Kazan told me that his new star was constantly asking about me, and seemed bent on patterning his acting technique and life after me, or at least on the person he thought I was after seeing *The Wild One*. But when I met Jimmy, he had a simplicity that I found endearing.'[5]

Kazan led Brando across the set to introduce him. 'Jimmy was nervous, and made it clear that he was not only mimicking my acting but also what he believed was my lifestyle. . . . But he had everything going for him, with a personality and presence that made audiences curious, as well as looks and a vulnerability that women especially found appealing.'[6]

The cameras finally finished rolling on *East of Eden* on 9 August 1954, leaving James Dean physically exhausted yet mentally exhilarated. He knew he had pulled off a major triumph, and the reviews confirmed it.

In the *New York Times* the respected critic Bosley Crowther wrote: 'This young actor, who is here doing his first big screen stint, is a mass of histrionic gingerbread. He scuffs his feet, he whirls, he pouts, he sputters, he leans against walls, he rolls his eyes, he swallows his words – all like Marlon Brando used to.' Thus a star was born.

Now came the accolades, the pot of gold at the end of a long rainbow. Jo Van Fleet won an Academy

Award for best supporting actress in her role as the long-suffering mother. James Dean received an Oscar nomination, as did Kazan and playwright Osborn.

Behind the scenes, the Warner Bros publicity machine was at full throttle. With the guiding hand of Dean's agent Dick Clayton to offer advice, they decided to use their new asset for maximum results to promote a movie that on the face of it was not blockbuster material. The easy way in those days to propel an actor into the columns was to find him a romantic link. James Dean had to be a romantic leading man – with an edge, to be sure, but the dream boyfriend that college girls and their mothers across America could embrace in their fantasies.

Enter a young beauty named Pier Angeli, a sultry Sicilian-born actress cutting a niche for herself as a fragile heroine in pot-boilers with titles like *The Devil Makes Three* and *The Flame and the Flesh*. Later that year she would marry singer Vic Damone, a marriage that lasted a mere four years, and she would die of an overdose of barbiturates in 1971 at the age of thirty-nine.

But this was the up-and-coming young actress that the powers-that-be decreed should become James Dean's girlfriend, reinforcing the image they needed of a man who was virile, macho, and heterosexual.

The media latched on to it, giving their readers voracious chapter and verse of a romance made in heaven. As one gossip columnist put it: 'James Dean has the lead in *East of Eden*, and you'll be hearing about him soon. Pier Angeli, who isn't in the movie, has discovered him already.'[7] But the odd fact was that Jimmy and Pier did fall in love in their own way – she starry-eyed and romantic, he respecting her as a friend, and neither of them ever admitting that they actually went to bed together.

But for months they were seen out on the town, laughing and flirting, even buying gold 'friendship rings' for each other at a Beverly Hills jewellery store. In those innocent days of the fifties, it was simply called 'dating'.

During this heady time, their favourite watering hole became the Villa Capri, an Italian restaurant that was the haunt of Frank Sinatra and his crowd, as well as the celebrated gangster Mickey Cohen and *his* friends. Stars like Johnny Weissmuller would appear, giving his famous Tarzan yell whenever he walked in, much to the amusement of the customers. Jimmy and Pier shared their personal booth number six, and over pasta and white wine the romance for all the world appeared to blossom.

The liaison faltered and broke up because of the intervention of Mama Pierangeli, a devout Catholic who decided she wanted a more stable figure for a potential son-in-law.

Pier dutifully started dating other men, while Jimmy valiantly kept his name in the papers with a variety of starlets on his arm, among them the pert Terry Moore who accompanied him to the premiere of *Sabrina* at the Paramount Theatre. The last time Jimmy and Pier were seen in public together was at another premiere, of the James Mason–Judy Garland saga *A Star is Born* – and days later Pier was gone from his life, engaged and later married to Vic Damone.

Quite what went on behind the scenes has never been revealed, but it was widely reported that Jimmy was 'heart-broken' when she left him, and for ever after Pier would be reviled as the scarlet lady who had been the one true love of his life, and spurned him.

Perhaps to get over the split, Jimmy buried himself in work. Numerous TV plays kept him busy, and he became a close friend of another powerful

Method actor, Rod Steiger. 'I was one of the few people for whom he seemed to have some respect,' Steiger would recall. 'He was surrounded by a lot of individuals I call the "grey people", weird groups. There is a terrible phrase called "going Hollywood" – and I think that's what happened to Jimmy.'[8]

Marlon Brando, too, was finding the eager young actor constantly at his elbow, even if that meant being on the end of a phone. 'He would call me and ask advice or suggest a night out. He regarded me as a kind of older brother or mentor, and I suppose I responded to him as if I was. But we never became really close.'[9]

At this time, Winton Dean was interviewed by the movie magazine *Modern Screen*, and gave a revealing insight into his relationship with his son. 'My Jim is a tough boy to understand,' he said. 'At least he is for me. But maybe that's because I don't understand actors. Jim and I – we never had that closeness. Now he lives in a world I don't understand too well, the actor's world. But he's a good boy, my Jim, and I'm very proud of him. My boy will make his mark.'

Now came the film that would make that mark, immortalising James Dean in the minds and hearts of millions of youngsters of his generation and for generations to come. *Rebel Without a Cause* had been a book written by a prison psychiatrist named Robert M. Lindner, first published in 1944. Warner Bros had paid $5,000 to option it for a movie, and it had languished on the shelves for a decade. But now, at last, it was about to be dusted off and reach the screen.

SEVEN

REBEL WITHOUT A CAUSE

R*ebel Without a Cause* was originally conceived as a modest black-and-white B-movie on the lines of *Blackboard Jungle*, a teen-oriented MGM drama notable for its pulsating rock 'n roll soundtrack, with 'Rock Around the Clock' from Bill Haley and the Comets setting the pace and tone behind the opening titles for a riveting drama that never let the tension falter. It was making a mint at the box-office, with youngsters queueing round the block to see Glenn Ford as a teacher struggling to win the respect of his juvenile delinquent pupils in a tough slum school – with a young Sidney Poitier as the gang leader. 'My pupils are the kind you don't turn your back on, even in class!' was one memorable quote.

Warner Bros recognised that this could be the start of a cycle, and decided to jump on the bandwagon, fast, with their own film about disaffected American youth – but seen from the young people's point of view. Director Nicholas Ray and screenwriter Stewart Stern had travelled throughout America interviewing police officers, judges, youth leaders and juvenile welfare officials to collect material for the movie. They had met members of a teenage gang first-hand, and spent hours in the Los Angeles Juvenile Court watching, listening, and making notes.

The director insisted that all the characters should be based on actual cases, with the parents (played by Jim Backus and Ann Doran) being the ones 'put on trial' and, in the end, found guilty. It was a new slant to an age-old problem, and in James Dean the director knew he had found the actor he wanted to play the leading role of seventeen-year-old Jim Stark, tortured, rebellious, desperately craving love from parents for whom he had lost all respect. 'Jimmy was a model of adolescence in general and American adolescence in particular,' Ray said. 'He was someone who symbolised the doubts and aspirations of his generation.'[1]

Filming began at the Burbank Studios on 28 March 1955. Four days later Warner Bros scrapped the footage already in the can. Jack L. Warner, the formidable studio boss, personally ordered the film to be reshot — in colour, CinemaScope, and with a lot more money swelling the budget. The reason behind this unprecedented, but, to the film-makers, highly gratifying, move was the release of *East of Eden* and the realisation that they had the hottest star in Hollywood under their roof.

James Dean did not let them down. He delivered an excoriating portrayal of alienated youth, set against a compelling mixture of family conflict, social commentary, and potential violence.

There were two other key parts: Plato, a young teenager who becomes obsessed with Stark, and Judy, flowering into womanhood with an over-protective father causing her problems at home.

For Plato, the director chose Sal Mineo, aged only sixteen, who had graced the Broadway stage (in *The Rose Tattoo* and as the young prince in *The King and I*) and whose dark, sensitive features disguised his background as a trouble-maker who had been expelled from school at the age of eight, and who would be stabbed to death at the age of thirty-five in a downtown Hollywood alley.

For Judy, he selected Natalie Wood, daughter of a Russian architect and a French ballet dancer, a young doe-eyed beauty of seventeen who had been a child star from the age of five with her first screen role in *Happy Land*. Cynical observers were unkind enough to suggest that it was not her track record that won her the role of Jim Stark's girlfriend, but the fact that she was having an affair with the director that clinched it. Either way, Natalie went on to win a best supporting Oscar nomination, as did Sal Mineo. The only reason James Dean's name was left off the roll of honour was that he was already up for *East of Eden*.

Natalie herself would die in a boating accident when she was lost overboard from a yacht in 1981, fulfilling the bizarre coincidence of the leading trio in *Rebel* whose lives all ended in tragedy.

Whatever the strong emotions rampaging through the action on the screen, behind the cameras other currents were swirling. Reportedly, Natalie Wood fell head over heels for Jimmy — but then, so did Sal. The impressionable young teenager's attraction for his co-star became a virtual obsession, and after the movie was finished he would tell friends how he and Dean had enjoyed a physically intimate relationship, though insiders on the set considered the boast unlikely and mere fantasy. Interestingly, the word 'punk' was cut from the original screenplay: in those days it was slang for homosexual.

In fact the man in James Dean's complex personal life at that time was another young actor named Jack Simmons, who was a fixture on the Hollywood homosexual scene, and had worked in TV with Jimmy. His favourite hang-out was the Tropical Village club by the beach at Santa Monica, a popular gay venue where show-business personalities of that persuasion would gather, secure in the knowledge that their secret was safe from the prying eyes of outsiders, particularly the media. It would be no surprise to find Rock Hudson sashaying round the dance floor with another rugged leading man of that time, George Nader, in his arms, while other familiar faces dropping by might include Anthony Perkins, Tab Hunter – and James Dean.

The libel laws deterred the gossip columnists from unsheathing their claws, and even the raunchy tabloids had to content themselves with suggestive headlines like: 'The Simple Life of a Busy

Bachelor', 'Rock Hudson Gets Rich Alone' or 'Scared of Marriage, Rock?'

Finally the studios started to worry that 'the Rock' might start losing his fans, which would mean dollars down the drain if the box-office dried up. So they arranged for Hudson to marry Phyllis Gates, a studio secretary, making sure of massive media coverage for the event and even allowing pictures to be taken of the happy couple kissing and cuddling in their honeymoon bedroom suite. It was a cosmetic exercise, and it worked brilliantly. Rock was accepted as a 'straight guy' – and his fans reckoned that it was just bad luck when he and Phyllis were divorced a year later. Hudson died of AIDS in 1985.

For James Dean, the studios were equally anxious to keep romance in the air, contrived or consummated, whether it was with his co-star Natalie Wood or, indeed, the earlier fling with Pier Angeli. There would also be a 'close relationship' with Ursula Andress, seven years before the Swiss beauty made her big international impact in the first James Bond thriller *Dr No*.

In fact Jimmy had moved in with Jack Simmons, and they were living together in an apartment near the studios. It was at this time that Jimmy, now financially independent, bought himself two expensive items: a white Ford station wagon and a silver-grey 1500 cc Porsche Spyder convertible.

His fascination with speed from an early age had developed into a passion for motor racing, and this was his first genuine racing car. On 26 March, two days before the cameras were due to roll on *Rebel*, he entered the Palm Springs Road Races, and came second in the finals. In a bar afterwards, someone asked him why he would risk his neck at this crucial stage in his career, with everything to live for. His reply was significant, and in hindsight tragically profound. 'If you're afraid to die, there's no room in your life to make discoveries,'[2] was all he said.

Since *Rebel Without a Cause* was the one film that placed James Dean on a plateau and affected generations of teenagers around the world, it is instructive to look more closely at the ingredients that created a shock effect little short of mass hysteria. There was Jim Stark's relationship with his mother, for a start. Both parents came from well-to-do, middle-class suburbia, living in comfort and financial security.

But behind the lace curtains his father was a hen-pecked weakling, and his mother used emotional blackmail to bring her son to order: 'Remember how I almost died giving birth to you' she shrieked in one of the film's most highly charged moments, to which Jim – or the real Jimmy perhaps – responded with a gut-wrenching scream: 'You're tearing me apart!' in what has been called one of the cinema's great cries of anguish.

Another unforgettable scene was the 'chicken run', when Jim had been challenged by Buzz, an arrogant rival, to a duel with stolen cars fought out on a clifftop at night, the drivers racing to the edge and jumping out seconds before the cars hurtle over on to the rocks far below. The first to jump would be 'chicken'.

Jim Stark changes into a a white T-shirt, blue jeans and a red nylon windcheater for the contest – oddly enough, the same gear James Dean wore for his final, fateful drive months later and that would be copied by teenagers the world over. In the dramatic race, his rival's sleeve becomes caught in the door handle and Buzz (played by Corey Allen) is dragged, screaming, to his death.

Back home, frightened and distressed at the enormity of what has happened, Jim pleads with his parents: 'I've got to talk to somebody. I'm in trouble. Just once I want to do something right. Dad, stand up for me. *Stand up!*' He grabs his father by the lapels, and wrestles him across the room while his mother screams at them from the stairs. It was this scene, more than any other, that gave the film its X certificate when it opened in Britain.

Dean prepared for that crucial scene in his dressing-room, working himself up to an emotional pitch by playing the *Ride of the Valkyrie* at full volume – then striding out to the set to complete the scene in a single take, earning the applause of the crew and his fellow-stars at the end of it. It was Jim Backus, the father, who revealed afterwards that Jimmy had broken two small bones in his left hand with the intensity of the fight.

Sadly, James Dean never lived to see the performance that made him an icon. Warner Bros – by coincidence, not design – released the film the day after his death, and the posthumous reviews summed up the tragedy of a young life cut short before its time. Alan Brien of the London *Evening*

Standard wrote: 'James Dean, alas, is dead. But his ghost on the screen in what was only his second film will remain among the immortals of the cinema.'

William Whitebait said in the *New Statesman*: 'James Dean gives a performance wholly his own, more electric than any of Marlon Brando's,' while in the *Daily Sketch*, Harold Conway called the film 'a superb portrayal of youth's misdirected adolescence'. In the *Sunday Times* Dilys Powell added her own commendation: 'There has been no player of his or any other generation to rival his interpretation of the violent desperation of youth.'

But perhaps the ultimate tribute both to the film and to its star came from William Faulkner, who said: '*Rebel Without a Cause* will remain a masterpiece, because it is the American cinema's only Greek tragedy.'[3]

It was left to Marlon Brando to summarise most concisely the impact of James Dean upon youth culture. 'Like me, Jimmy became a symbol of social change by happenstance. *Rebel Without a Cause* was a story about a new lost generation of young people, and the reaction to it, like that to *The Wild One*, was a sign of the tremors beginning to quake beneath the surface of our culture. . . . He had a subtle energy and an intangible quality which had a tremendous impact on audiences. . . . The social fabric was being replaced by something new, for better or worse.'[4]

Meanwhile James Dean, aged twenty-four, went back to work with no hint of the personal, ultimate tragedy that was about to overwhelm him.

GIANT

*R*ebel wrapped on 26 May 1955. James Dean had only three days between finishing one film and starting another. *Giant* was the movie for which every actor in Hollywood would have given his eye-teeth and more for a role. In 1952 Edna Ferber's rambling family saga about cattle barons and oil wells in Texas had become an immediate bestseller, with more than twenty-five million copies sold over the next five years. Originally she refused to sell the film rights unless she was made one of the producers.

A year later Warner Bros finally acceded to Ferber's demands, and she joined the eminent director George Stevens (*Shane, A Place in the Sun*) on the credits. The massive project took two years in pre-production, spent another thirteen months in the editing rooms, and would last three hours seventeen minutes on the screen.

Stevens assembled a star cast with enormous box-office fire-power: Rock Hudson played the central figure of cattle rancher Bick Benedict, Elizabeth Taylor his spirited wife Leslie, with Dennis Hopper, Mercedes McCambridge, Carroll Baker and veteran Chill Wills in strong support.

But it was James Dean as the brooding, introvert farmhand Jett Rink who stole the scenes. Left a small slice of land and 'down to his last collar button', he strikes it rich in oil, and rises through the social strata to become the wealthiest mogul in the Lone Star State. Probably Dean's most telling moment is when he appears on the patio of the Benedict ranch, soaked in oil from the big gusher, to taunt his hated former boss with his good fortune. 'My well came in! I'm rich, I'm the richest, I'm going to have more money than you ever thought you could – you and the rest of all you stinking Benedicts!'

It is a compelling portrait of poverty leading to wealth and power, spanning three decades, and although his performance shows some cracks when Rink ages close to fifty, Dean won himself a second Academy Award nomination – while Stevens walked off with his second Oscar. Edna Ferber, watching the box-office dollars roll in, allowed: 'Jimmy was original. Impish, magnetic, utterly winning one moment, obnoxious the next. Definitely gifted. Frequently maddening.' It sounds like a telegram to St Peter at the Pearly Gates, warning him of the impending new arrival. Because now the clock was fast ticking away the last days of James Dean's life.

Although exhausted from *Rebel*, he went straight into his change of character, first with wardrobe and make-up tests, then on 3 June 1955 to join the cast and 120-strong film unit on location in the tiny Texas township of Marfa, hardly more than a speck on the map, where they would endure six long weeks in the broiling midsummer prairie heat.

The dust-filled main street boasted one grocery store, three cafés, and two bars, with a couple of motels and the El Paisano hotel just outside town where most of the unit stayed. The Palace cinema had been closed for three years – so not a lot was going on by way of entertainment.

Stevens found a private house for Dean, Rock Hudson, and Chill Wills to share, shrewdly calculating that the stifling proximity would ignite the personal friction and animosity he wanted from them in the movie. His Machiavellian plan succeeded. The trio spent long hours around a poker table in the modest front room drinking Lone Star beer and scoring verbal points off each other – and it was almost a relief to transfer their hostility to their roles next day in front of the cameras.

The exhausting location was not helped by the fact that the grizzled, tough-talking Stevens, now fifty-one and in his prime, insisted on shooting every scene from innumerable angles, knowing he would achieve the result he wanted in the editing rooms.

He also demanded that his actors stayed in make-up all day, every day – even if they were not likely to be used – which led to a further battle of wills with his volatile young star. Stevens would later pass the acerbic comment: 'All in all it was a hell of a headache to work with Jimmy. He was always pulling and hauling, and he had developed a cultivated, designed irresponsibility.'[1]

Physically, James Dean came through an arduous location surprisingly well, given the pressure of making an epic-scale movie, behind-the-scenes tensions, and the fact that every day they were watched by virtually the entire population of Marfa, sometimes up to a thousand onlookers, who made the daily trek out to the Benedict ranch that had been built for the film, and stood behind police barriers to gawp at the actors.

Jimmy was under strict doctor's orders to stay on a high-protein diet, which helped. But the emotional flaws showed through, and those closest to him were the first to notice. Both Elizabeth Taylor and Mercedes McCambridge took him under their wing like protective mother hens – indeed, they were referred to as 'surrogate mothers' by the crew.

Liz would sit up talking with him into the early hours, later revealing: 'Jimmy would tell me about his past life, the grief and unhappiness he had experienced, and some of his loves and tragedies.'[2] Mercedes – now thirty-five, intense and vibrant, once called 'the world's greatest living radio actress' by Orson Welles, no less – would recall with a mixture of fondness and concern: 'I can't tell you how he wanted to be patted! Jimmy was the runt in a litter of thoroughbreds, and you could feel the loneliness beating out of him.'[3]

Of such a volatile mix was *Giant* created, and completed on 21 September, with just over a year in the cutting rooms to come. The climactic final scene in the saga takes place in an empty ballroom. The occasion is the formal opening of the Jett Rink Airport and Hotel Emperador, with everyone who was anyone in Texas society invited. Rink's motorcade sweeps up the street, but the millionaire host has been drinking and can barely walk in a straight line as he enters the packed ballroom to the tune of 'The Yellow Rose of Texas' from the orchestra.

When he is finally introduced, Jett is so inebriated he is unable to rise to his feet, and simply sinks back, burying his face on the table-cloth. The gilt-edged guest list evaporates in disgust, and Jett – with the sickening realisation that he has not a true friend in the world – finally makes his drunken speech to a sea of empty tables. 'Poor Jett . . . rich Mrs Benedict . . . she's beautiful, lovely, a woman a man wants . . . a woman a man's got to have.' Finally he collapses to the floor, dragging the table and its contents with him.

What most filmgoers never realised is that it was not James Dean's slurred voice delivering that last, oddly poignant speech. Stevens, ever the perfectionist, was not satisfied with Dean's delivery, but by then it was too late. Jimmy was dead, and the voice you hear belongs to another actor, Nick Adams.

Dean knew how to act drunk. An actress friend, Carol Easton, recalled how he was once taking private acting classes with Jeff Corey, a local coach who taught aspiring youngsters at his home, when he was given a particular exercise to enact.

'It was a scene for two college students sharing a room. Jimmy was required to tell his room-mate, who had a serious alcohol problem, to stop drinking because he was so worried about him. When Jimmy came out into the centre of the room he was acting drunk. We all thought he had misunderstood the instructions. Then the room-mate asked Jimmy why he was drunk, and Jimmy told him he was going to stay drunk until he promised to sober up. And that's how they played the scene. Neat twist!'[4]

By now James Dean was in serious demand. His money troubles were over, and he could concentrate on his career without worrying about where the next meal would come from. His current agent, Jane Deacy, was about to sign him with

MGM for the boxing drama *Somebody Up There Likes Me* – the role that would eventually go to Paul Newman. The film won two Oscars. She was negotiating a new contract with Warner Bros that would earn her client a staggering $100,000 a picture – he had been paid $10,000 for *East of Eden*, $15,000 for *Rebel Without a Cause* and $20,000 for *Giant*. Their blue-eyed boy was rich and running.

It was now that Dean invested a heap of those dollars into his new toy – the small silver-grey Porsche Spyder 550, built for speed rather than strength with its vulnerable aluminium body and ladder frame, but with a four-cam air-cooled four-cylinder engine mounted in the middle and with a top speed upwards of 120 mph. But there was one other vital component: the brakes had been widened, so that the driver could 'stop on a dime'. Jimmy bought the racing car from Competition Motors, trading in his own Porsche Speedster 365 in part-exchange, plus $7,000 on top. Only seventy-eight cars in that new supermodel were built and sold that year, and immediately he had an artist friend paint 130, his racing number, in black on the bonnet and sides. And on the tail, the name he had given his prized possession: *The Little Bastard*.

Then he looked around for somewhere to race. There was a competition on 1 October up in Salinas, a small town in the San Joaquin Valley some 300 miles north of Los Angeles where he had filmed location scenes in *East of Eden*. With his friend and mechanic Rolf Weutherich, aged twenty-eight, to help and advise, he decided to enter.

Two days before setting off, Jimmy was relaxing over dinner at the Villa Capri, sitting out in the warm autumn sunshine, when Alec Guinness walked by with a friend, writer Thelma Moss. The British actor was in Hollywood filming *The Swan* with Grace Kelly – and on this particular evening he was surprised to find his sleeve seized by Jimmy, who insisted that he accompanied him into the car park to view his new trophy.

Guinness, ever the gentleman, acceded. But when his eye fell on the low-slung supercharged racer, he frowned. 'Please,' he said abruptly. 'Never drive it. If you get in that car you will be found dead in it by this time next week!'[5] Jimmy dismissed the warning with a short laugh, then invited the pair to be his guests for dinner. Later, Guinness would never be able to explain the extraordinary presentiment – except that it happened.

One final savage irony that fate decreed in the life, career, and premature death of James Dean happened as he prepared for the big race: he had agreed to film a TV public service commercial for the US National Safety Council. Playing himself, casually smoking a cigarette, wearing a cowboy outfit from *Giant* and indulging in a spot of rope twirling with a lasso, he had a 30-second conversation in an office with dark-suited actor Gig Young.

'How fast will your car go?' Gig began.

Jimmy sat back in a chair. 'A hundred-six, maybe seven.'

'Well,' Gig went on, 'We probably have a great many young people watching our show tonight, and for their benefit I'd like your opinion about fast driving on the highway. Do you think it's a good idea?'

'I took a lot of unnecessary chances on the highway,' Jimmy responded. 'I used to fly around quite a bit. Then I studied racing, and now I'm extra cautious because no-one knows what other people are doing half the time. You don't know what the next guy is going to do. On the track there are a lot of people who spend a lot of time developing rules and ways of safety. But I don't have the urge to speed on the highway. People say racing is dangerous, but I'll take my chances on the track any day rather than on a highway.'

As he stands to go, Gig asks him: 'One more question, Jimmy. Do you have any special advice for the young people driving?'

Dean looks straight into camera. 'Take it easy driving. The life you save might be mine.' And he gestures at himself with one thumb, and walks out.

James Dean was living in a small log cabin-style house at 14611 Sutton Street, in the San Fernando Valley, which he rented for $250 a month from Nikko Romanos, the Italian maitre d' at the Villa Capri. On 30 September 1955 Jimmy changed into white T-shirt, blue jeans and a red windbreaker, donned sunglasses, and went out to meet his friends Rolf the engineer, Bill Hickman, a stunt-car driver, and photographer Sandy Roth. At 1.30 p.m. they set off for Salinas on Route 99 (now 5), Jimmy at the wheel of his beloved new Porsche with Rolf sitting beside him, the others following in a station wagon.

At 3.00 p.m. they stopped at Tip's Diner to have a snack and a glass of milk. At 3.30 p.m., south of

Bakersfield, Jimmy was pulled up by a highway patrolman, Otie V. Hunter, and told he had been doing 65 mph in a 55 mph area. He was given a ticket, signed for it, and drove on – without the officer recognising who he was booking. But the patrolman noted on the form that the weather was 'clear' and the road conditions 'good'.

At Wasco, they turned off Route 99 on to Highway 466, heading west into the setting sun. Shortly after, Jimmy spotted a petrol station – and a familiar face, which belonged to Lance Reventlow, aged nineteen, the son of heiress Barbara Hutton. They chatted together, and Jimmy boasted how on one straight stretch of road he had just touched 130 mph in his new car. True or not, he was driving fast that day.

They took off again, approaching Cholame along the arrow-straight road through the Polonia Pass, where it was tempting for any driver to put his foot down and zip through the endless terrain. Night comes swiftly to the desert. The sun had dropped lower in the sky behind the parched brown hills, flooding the valley with a blinding light that would dazzle any driver coming from the east.

It happened at the intersection of 466 and the turn-off into Highway 41, which for approaching vehicles meant crossing the road in front of oncoming traffic. A large two-tone black-and-white Ford sedan suddenly turned into the Porsche's path.

The driver, a college student at California Polytechnic named Donald Gene Turnupseed, a year younger than Jimmy, would swear at the inquest that he never saw the silver-grey Porsche hurtling at him at a speed that has been estimated at well over 100 mph. James Dean's last words as the heavy vehicle inexorably pulled across into his side of the road were: 'That guy's got to see us. He's got to stop!'[6] But the Ford trundled on, slowing to a halt. Instead of braking, Jimmy stamped on the accelerator to swerve around the other car – but his instincts were too late.

The Spyder slammed into the Ford, careered off the road and ended up a mangled wreck close to a telegraph pole. The Ford slid on, and stopped. The driver had superficial bruises.

The impact threw Rolf into a nearby field. Jimmy would have followed, but his feet were jammed beneath the clutch and brake pedals, and his neck was broken instantly. The death certificate confirmed multiple fractures and internal injuries.

The inquest cleared Turnupseed, and put the onus on Jimmy for driving too fast, though when it came to who-blames-whom, questions were asked as to why the student had slowed instead of accelerating into the junction if he had not seen Dean. Rolf went home to Germany, but never fully recovered from the accident, and in 1981 was himself killed at the wheel of his car after losing control on a wet road and crashing into a wall.

James Dean died intestate, with Winton inheriting the proceeds from his son's accident insurance and personal belongings, totalling in all $96,000. *Rebel Without a Cause* opened the day after Dean's death, and the box-office tills started ringing.

Jimmy's casket made the same sad journey from Los Angeles to Fairmount that his mother's had done only fifteen years previously, and on 8 October he was buried in Back Creek cemetery, close to the home where he spent the happy, eager, expectant days of his youth. Elizabeth Taylor and Edna Ferber sent flowers, and a wreath came from the cast of *Giant*. Dr James DeWeerd, now minister

at a tabernacle in Indianapolis, joined local preacher
Xen Harvey to conduct the service.

It was the largest funeral ever seen in Fairmount,
with more than three thousand mourners crowding
into the chapel and overflowing into the churchyard
outside.

NINE

AFTERWARDS

I f death corrodes the flesh, so it purifies the myth –
and this was never more true than with the death
of James Dean. On similar lines, Marlon Brando
said that we can only guess what kind of actor
Jimmy would have become in another twenty years;
instead he died, and was forever entombed in
his myth.

With his death came waves of hysteria, and not
all from teenagers. For three years Warner Bros
received two thousand letters a week from bereaved
fans, and even today they keep coming. *Giant's*
release thirteen months after the star died spawned
fresh adulation, and films like *Come Back to the Five
and Dime, Jimmy Dean, Jimmy Dean* (1982),
documentaries like Robert Altman's *The James Dean
Story* (1957), *James Dean – the First American Teenager*
(1976) and *Forever James Dean* (1988), even *Badlands*
(1974), with Martin Sheen as a Dean lookalike, all
helped to keep the legend alive.

There was also a surge in memorabilia, from movie posters to monogrammed T-shirts. Less salubrious were other mementos — like pieces of metal, supposedly from his crashed Porsche, on sale. Most ghoulish of all, the twisted shell of the mangled car was put on show in Los Angeles for fans to clamber over and, for a dollar more, to sit in the blood-stained driving seat.

But every year in the last week of September, a James Dean Festival brings Fairmount alive for three noisy days, with a 'cinethon' of his films showing at the town hall (there is still no cinema), lookalikes roaming down Main Street and vintage car rallies trundling through the town.

Over in California, something more bizarre takes place. On 30 September, the 'James Dean Death Drive' sets off from Los Angeles down Route 99 in a convoy of vintage cars, some of them replicas of Jimmy's Porsche.

Many of the drivers wear white T-shirts, blue jeans and red zip-up windcheaters. They will stop at Tip's Diner for a glass of milk, just as Jimmy did, and again on the highway south of Bakersfield, where patrolman Hunter pulled Jimmy over to give him a ticket, and at the place where their idol died they gather at 5.45 p.m. precisely to say a prayer for Jimmy.

The spot is marked by a chromium memorial built around a nearby tree by a Japanese businessman named Seita Ohnishi, a monument not particularly aesthetic but impressive all the same. He spent $200,000 on it in 1983 because, he said, he found it distressing that no American had bothered to mark the spot.

At the time the unexpected benefactor told the world: 'There are some things, like the hatred that accompanies war, that are best forgotten. There are others, like the love inspired by this young actor, that should be preserved for all time.'[1]

EPILOGUE

Many fans refused to accept their idol's death.

From 1955, documentaries continued to be made about his life. Among them: *The James Dean Story* (1957, dir. Robert Altman), *Idol — the Story of James Dean* (1975, dir. Ray Connolly), *Hollywood: The Rebels: 'James Dean'* (1982, dir. Claudio Masenza), *Forever James Dean* (1998, dir. Ara Cheymayan), *Bye Bye Jimmy* (1990, dir. Paul Watson), *James Dean: the Race with Destiny* (1997, dir. Mardi Rustan).

Other tributes include *To Climb Steep Hills* (TV, 1962), *Badlands* (film, 1974), *September 30 1955* (film, 1977), *Dean* (stage musical, 1977), *Come Back to the Five and Dime, Jimmy Dean, Jimmy Dean* (stage and film, 1982).

The death of James Dean spawned a myth which still exists to this day.

NOTES

CHAPTER ONE

1. Paul Alexander, *Boulevard of Broken Dreams*, p. 19

CHAPTER TWO

1. Joe Hyams, *James Dean, Little Boy Lost*, p. 12
2. Alexander, *Boulevard of Broken Dreams*, p. 32
3. Ibid, p. 34
4. Hyams, *James Dean, Little Boy Lost*, p. 16
5. Ibid, p. 19
6. Ibid, p. 21

CHAPTER THREE

1. Alexander, *Boulevard of Broken Dreams*, p. 56
2. Ibid, p. 69

CHAPTER FOUR

1. Hyams, *James Dean, Little Boy Lost*, p. 38
2. Ibid, p. 49
3. Ibid, p. 50
4. Ibid, p. 57
5. Ibid, p. 63

CHAPTER FIVE

1. Robert Tanitch, *The Unknown James Dean*, p. 20

Notes

2. Alexander, *Boulevard of Broken Dreams*, p. 108
3. Ibid, p. 109
4. Hyams, *James Dean, Little Boy Lost*, p. 89
5. Ibid, p. 96
6. Ibid, p. 97
7. Ibid, p. 98

CHAPTER SIX

1. Elia Kazan, *Elia Kazan, A Life*, p. 142
2. Ibid, p. 144
3. Hyams, *James Dean, Little Boy Lost*, p. 130
4. Alexander, *Boulevard of Broken Dreams*, p. 148
5. Marlon Brando, *Songs My Mother Taught Me*, p. 220
6. Ibid, p. 220–1
7. Alexander, *Boulevard of Broken Dreams*, p. 150
8. Tom Hutchinson, *Rod Steiger*, p. 43
9. Joe Morella and Edward Z. Epstein, *Brando*, p. 59

CHAPTER SEVEN

1. Tanitch, *The Unknown James Dean*, p. 88
2. Alexander, *Boulevard of Broken Dreams*, p. 168
3. Tanitch, *The Unknown James Dean*, p. 101
4. Brando, *Songs My Mother Taught Me*, p. 221

CHAPTER EIGHT

1. Tanitch, *The Unknown James Dean*, p. 110
2. Hyams, *James Dean, Little Boy Lost*, p. 223
3. Ibid, p. 222
4. Alexander, *Boulevard of Broken Dreams*, p. 157

5. Hyams, *James Dean, Little Boy Lost*, p. 237
6. Alexander, *Boulevard of Broken Dreams*, p. 198

Chapter Nine

1. Hyams, *James Dean, Little Boy Lost*, p. 269

BIBLIOGRAPHY

Alexander, Paul, *James Dean, Boulevard of Broken Dreams*, Little, Brown & Company, London, 1994

Bast, William, *James Dean, a Biography*, Ballantine, New York, 1956

Bluttman, Susan, 'Rediscovering James Dean: The TV Legacy', in *Emmy*, 1990

Brando, Marlon, *Songs My Mother Taught Me*, Century, London, 1994

Gilmore, Jonathan, *The Real James Dean*, Pyramid, New York, 1975

Hopper, Hedda, *The Whole Truth and Nothing But*, with Brough, James, Doubleday, New York, 1963

Hutchinson, Tom, *Rod Steiger*, Victor Gollancz, London, 1998

Hyams, Joe, *James Dean, Little Boy Lost*, Century, London, 1993

Kazan, Elia, *Elia Kazan: A Life*, Knopf, New York, 1988

McCambridge, Mercedes, *The Quality of Mercy*, Times Books, New York, 1981

Morella, Joe and Epstein, Edward Z. *Brando*, Thomas Nelson & Sons, London, 1973

Tanitch, Robert, *The Unknown James Dean*, B.T. Batsford, London, 1997

POCKET BIOGRAPHIES

AVAILABLE

Beethoven
Anne Pimlott Baker

Ellen Terry
Moira Shearer

Mao Zedong
Delia Davin

David Livingstone
C.S. Nicholls

Scott of the Antarctic
Michael De-la-Noy

Abraham Lincoln
H.G. Pitt

Alexander the Great
E.E. Rice

**Marie and Pierre
Curie**
John Senior

Sigmund Freud
Stephen Wilson

Margot Fonteyn
Alastair Macaulay

Marilyn Monroe
Sheridan Morley and
Ruth Leon

Enid Blyton
George Greenfield

Rasputin
Harold Shukman

Winston Churchill
Robert Blake

Jane Austen
Helen Lefroy

George IV
Michael De-la-Noy

For a copy of our complete list or details of other Sutton titles, please contact Emma Leitch at Sutton Publishing Limited, Phoenix Mill, Thrupp, Stroud, Gloucestershire, GL5 2BU

POCKET BIOGRAPHIES

AVAILABLE

Christopher Wren
James Chambers

Che Guevara
Andrew Sinclair

W.G. Grace
Donald Trelford

The Brontës
Kathryn White

Lawrence of Arabia
Jeremy Wilson

Christopher Columbus
Peter Riviere

Martin Luther King
Harry Harmer

Genghis Khan
James Chambers

James Dean
William Hall

Cleopatra
E.E. Rice

John Ruskin
Francis O'Gorman

For a copy of our complete list or details of other Sutton titles, please contact Emma Leitch at Sutton Publishing Limited, Phoenix Mill, Thrupp, Stroud, Gloucestershire, GL5 2BU

POCKET BIOGRAPHIES

FORTHCOMING

Joseph Stalin
Harold Shukman

Juan and Eva Perón
Clive Foss

Queen Victoria
Elizabeth Longford

Lord Byron
Catherine Peters

Anthony Trollope
Graham Handley

For a copy of our complete list or details of other Sutton titles, please contact Emma Leitch at Sutton Publishing Limited, Phoenix Mill, Thrupp, Stroud, Gloucestershire, GL5 2BU